DAILY LIGHT

GRATITUDE JOURNAL

WRITTEN BY JOANNA HUNTER
ILLUSTRATED & FORMATTED BY STEPHANIE WICKER-CAMPBELL

MUSE ORACLE PRESS

The information in this book/journal should not be used as a substitute for medical or mental health advice. Always consult a medical or mental health practitioner when in need. The intent of the author is only to offer information of a general nature to help you create actionable steps, clarity, and momentum in your goals for the future. In the event you use any of the information in this book/journal for yourself, the author and publisher assume no responsibility or liability for your actions.

ISBN: 978-0-6458850-5-7

First Edition 2024 Authored by Joanna Hunter

Cover design and formatting by Stephanie Wicker-Campbell

Published by Muse Oracle Press Pty Ltd

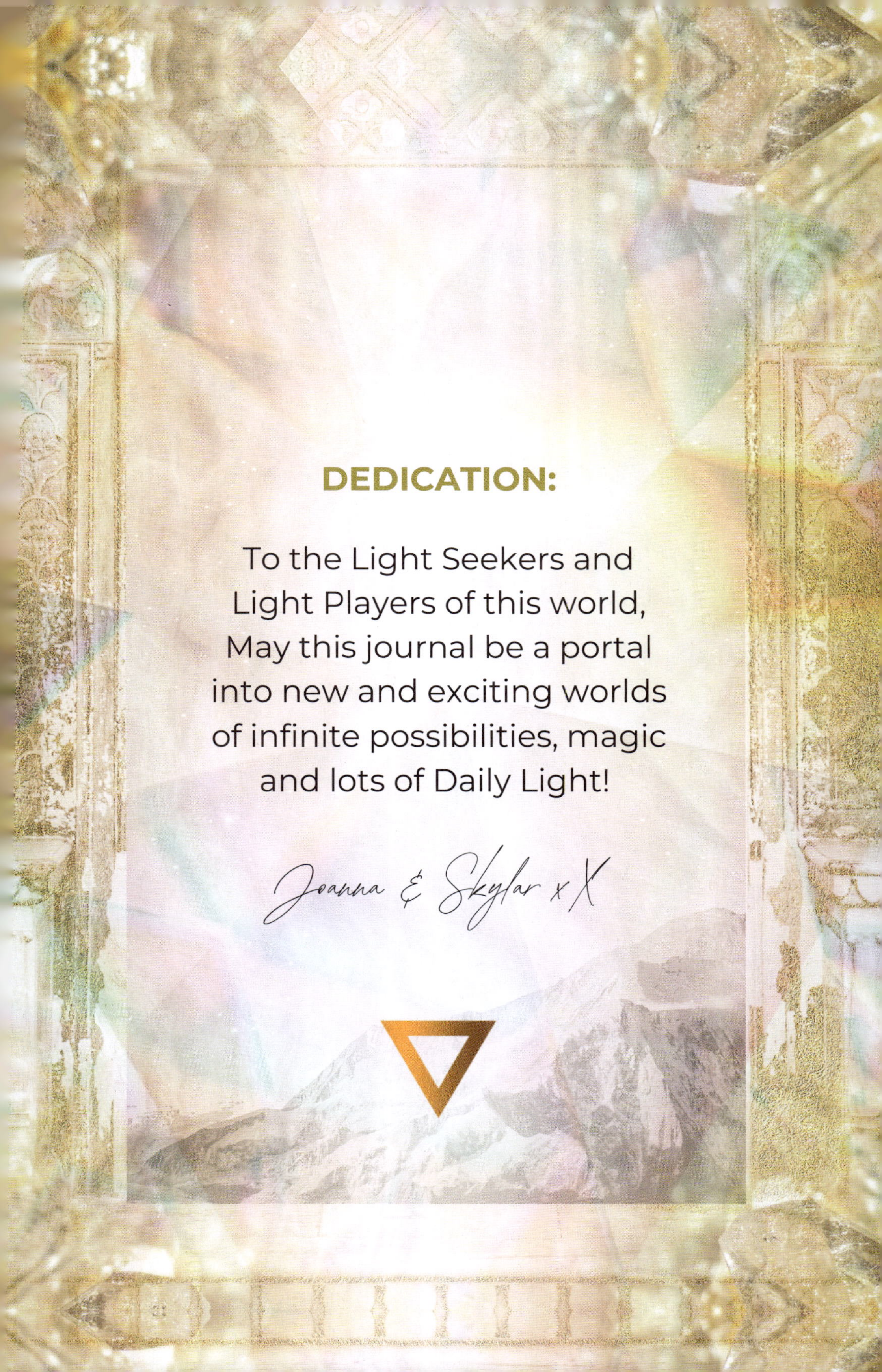

DEDICATION:

To the Light Seekers and
Light Players of this world,
May this journal be a portal
into new and exciting worlds
of infinite possibilities, magic
and lots of Daily Light!

Joanna & Skylar x X

DAILY
LIGHT

This journal belongs to:

In this journal I will create magic and set these sacred intentions:

"I AM Magic Incarnate."

Foreword

Hey Light Player,

Let's open our hearts to more Daily▽Light and abundance with the transcendent power of gratitude and affirmations!

It is my heartfelt hope that this journal is the answer for anyone who has ever been caught in the 'Ego Trap' and said the words, "I will be happy when ________." (fill in the blank of your choice).

This is an egoic delay tactic of massive proportions that shelves the receiving of more light now for later. Funny thing is that it's never later, it's always now o'clock. This leaves you out of the loop of your own happiness.

We think when we have the car of our dreams, the life partner we want, the big house, the job we desire, making the money we only once dreamed of, the perfect body, the Instagram worthy holidays... (I could go on but you get the idea), we will finally be happy. Here's the simple straight up truth, you won't be happier, not even close!

Here's why; Happiness is a feeling, not a thing. When we are happy, we are grateful. Happiness creates the feeling of gratitude inside us.

I once had the law of attraction teacher, the author Babel Mohr say to me; "Joanna if you can't be grateful for what you have, what makes you think you will be happier with more?"

That question changed my life. It hit me over the head like a two-by-four at first, but it changed my life! I mistakenly thought a semblance of happiness lay in having more stuff such as the "dream house", like I was Barbie or something!

I filled my life with what the magazines told me I should have, with all the stuff I once wanted because I believed my lack of happiness was a lack of something physical. In the moment of hearing that question, I realised I did not have a lack of stuff, but I did have a rather serious case of a lack of gratitude.

You see, happiness is an intangible thing. It's a smile from a baby, a random act of kindness from a stranger, a hug between two people at an airport that makes you believe in love, the sun on your face, a joke shared with good friends.

All those things can and will make us happy. Why? because all of those things bring us Daily Light and into the present moment where our true power lies. All too often our thoughts hang out in places where we are powerless, in the past making us depressed as it has already happened so we have no power there, or in the future making us anxious because it has not happened yet, therefore again there is no power there for us to draw on. Only the present moment has that power to connect us to Source.

Gratitude connects us to the Daily ▽ Light. The more we can connect to our Daily Light, the happier we become and the more present we become in our lives - NOW.

"Gratitude is the key."

Daily Light & infinite blessings,

Joanna & Skylar x X

Gratitude for the past
"YOU CAN'T REACH FOR ANYTHING NEW IF YOUR HANDS ARE STILL FULL OF YESTERDAY'S JUNK."
-LOUISE SMITH

Dearest Soul,

Skylar teaches we are a sacred vessel that is always maxed to capacity! Just like a cup can only be filled to the brim, so can we. Since we are always at capacity for what our vessels can hold because the universe is always giving, if we want new experiences we need to have a bit of a clear out.

This concept is the metaphysical reason why decluttering and forgiveness are such powerful spiritual practices and why they have become so popular in recent years because, simply put, they work!

In this section, we will explore Daily Light by letting go of the past through the lens of gratitude and forgiveness. I'll share some of my favourite affirmations from the Daily Light Affirmation Deck, turning your past into pure power and creating the space for newness in your life!

Joanna xX

I am so grateful for the experiences that shaped me into who I am today...

I am thankful for all my blessings that were once disguised as divine assignments and challenges, for they have sculpted my path with purpose...

"Your past does not define you. You define yourself by what you are willing to give your power to." - Skylar

I express gratitude for the opportunities that I had the courage to seize...

“I have deep gratitude for my past, as a point of reference not as my home address, because I don’t live there any more than you do.” - Joanna Hunter

I LOVE & ACCEPT
MYSELF WHOLLY
AND COMPLETELY

In my humble thanks, I give gratitude to the difficult people from my past who taught me much about myself...

I am sincerely thankful for my own strength I now choose to see in these memories...

"The past is a place of reference, not a place of residence; the past is a place of learning, not a place of living." - Roy T Bennette

Gratefully, I recognise the sacred threads of gratitude woven into the intricate tapestry of my past...

“In this bright future, you can’t forget your past.” - Bob Marley

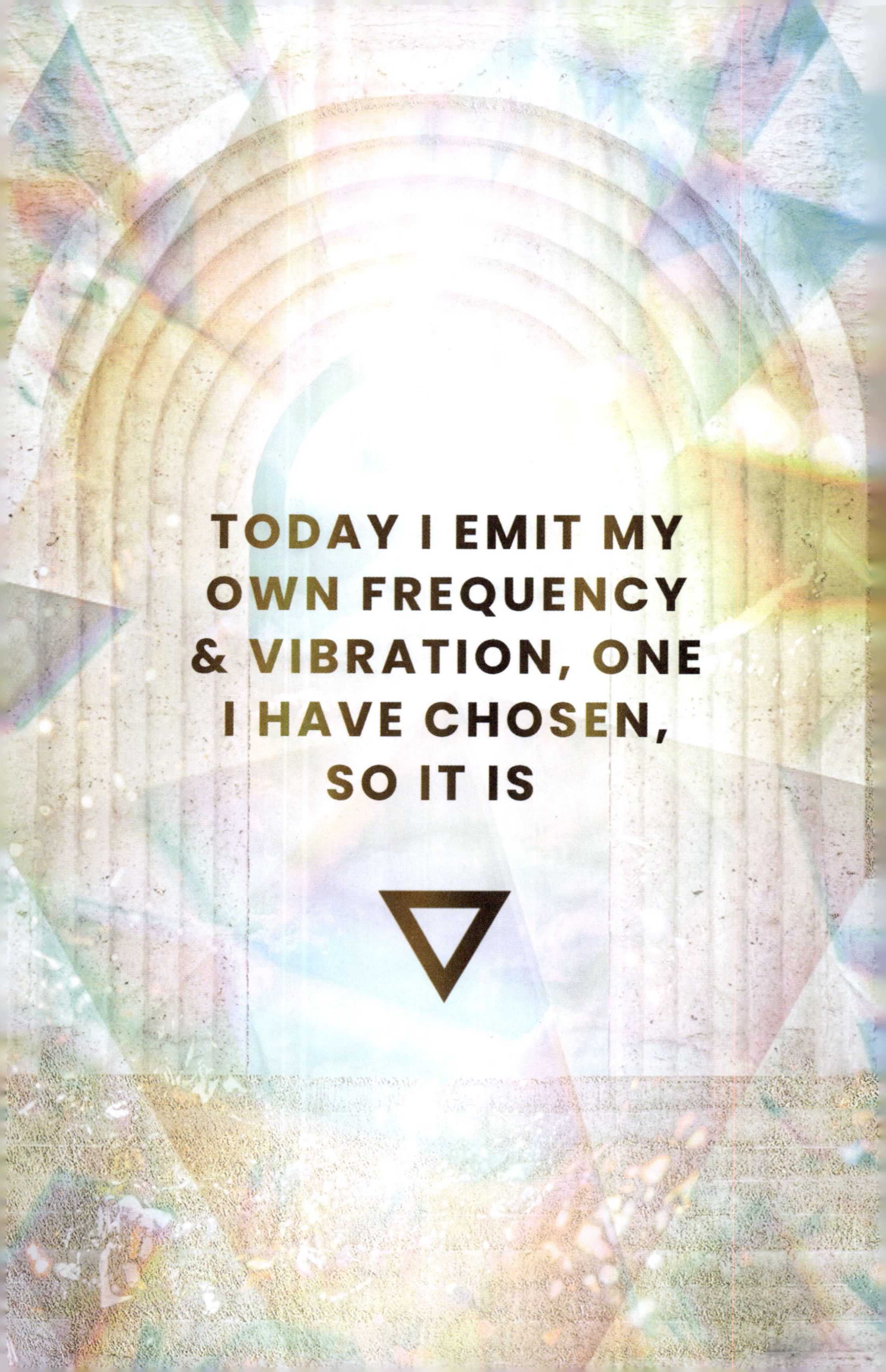
TODAY I EMIT MY
OWN FREQUENCY
& VIBRATION, ONE
I HAVE CHOSEN,
SO IT IS

With a grateful spirit, I honour myself by giving forgiveness to these things...

In heartfelt appreciation, I am thankful for these cherished memories that have become the tapestry of my life...

"You rock! You have a 100% track record of getting through life"
- Joanna Hunter

With humble heartfelt thanks, I embrace the past and its transformative influence on my journey in these ways...

“Gratitude makes sense of our past, brings peace for today, and creates a vision for tomorrow.” - Melody Beattie

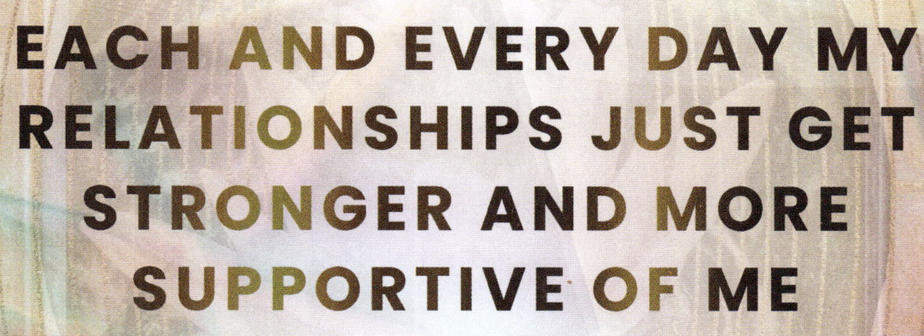
EACH AND EVERY DAY MY
RELATIONSHIPS JUST GET
STRONGER AND MORE
SUPPORTIVE OF ME

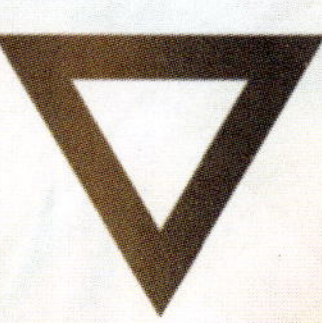

Gratitude radiates from my being as I acknowledge and let go of these difficult moments that linger from my past...

Reflecting on the past I invoke gratitude for the relationships that have enriched the fabric of my life...

"Forgiveness is not an occasional act; it is a constant attitude."
- Martin Luther King Jr.

I give gratitude for the people in my life that are no longer here...

“Forgiveness is the key to action and freedom.” - Maya Angelou

I ALWAYS
HAVE MORE
THAN ENOUGH
AND MORE IS
ALWAYS ON
THE WAY

In this sacred moment, I choose to receive all the Daily Light I missed from my past...

As I journey through time, I am deeply grateful for the serendipitous moments that painted my past with moments of magic like these...

"Forgiveness is a virtue of the brave." - Indira Gandhi

I gratefully forgive these perceived flaws and today I choose to love myself...

“In the face of full acceptance, forgiveness becomes obsolete.” - Skylar

I HAVE THE STRENGTH
I NEED TO FORGIVE
THOSE THAT NEED IT,
INCLUDING MYSELF

Gratitude for the lessons
life has taught us
"I AM STILL LEARNING."
-MICHELANGELO

Hey Sacred Magic Maker,

What if there was a magic sauce that made everything in your life taste better, even those hard lessons from the past, would you want it? What if this magic sauce was so brilliant it could cover the taste of life's most bitter experiences, even the ones we are still trying to unpack? What's more, this magic sauce is like my youngest child's definition of ketchup: it would make everything taste great! It could even guarantee that future experiences all tasted good naturally, would you want that magic sauce?

Well here's the recipe for magic sauce: Give daily gratitude!

I have lived a life with a lot of life lessons, at one time those life lessons made me feel victimised, hard done by and created the super unattractive "Woe is me" vibes in my body. Then Skylar taught me everything is data and all data has the power to propel us forward. In this moment I realised that even a bad experience has the power to be a life lesson, even if it just taught us that's not what we want, we can always be grateful for the lesson as all of those lessons have the power to propel us forward in life.

In this section, we give gratitude for the life lessons that have paved the way to this NOW moment...Let's juice the daily light from our experiences in those all-important life lessons.

I am so grateful for these life lessons...

I give sacred thanks for the lessons I learned today...

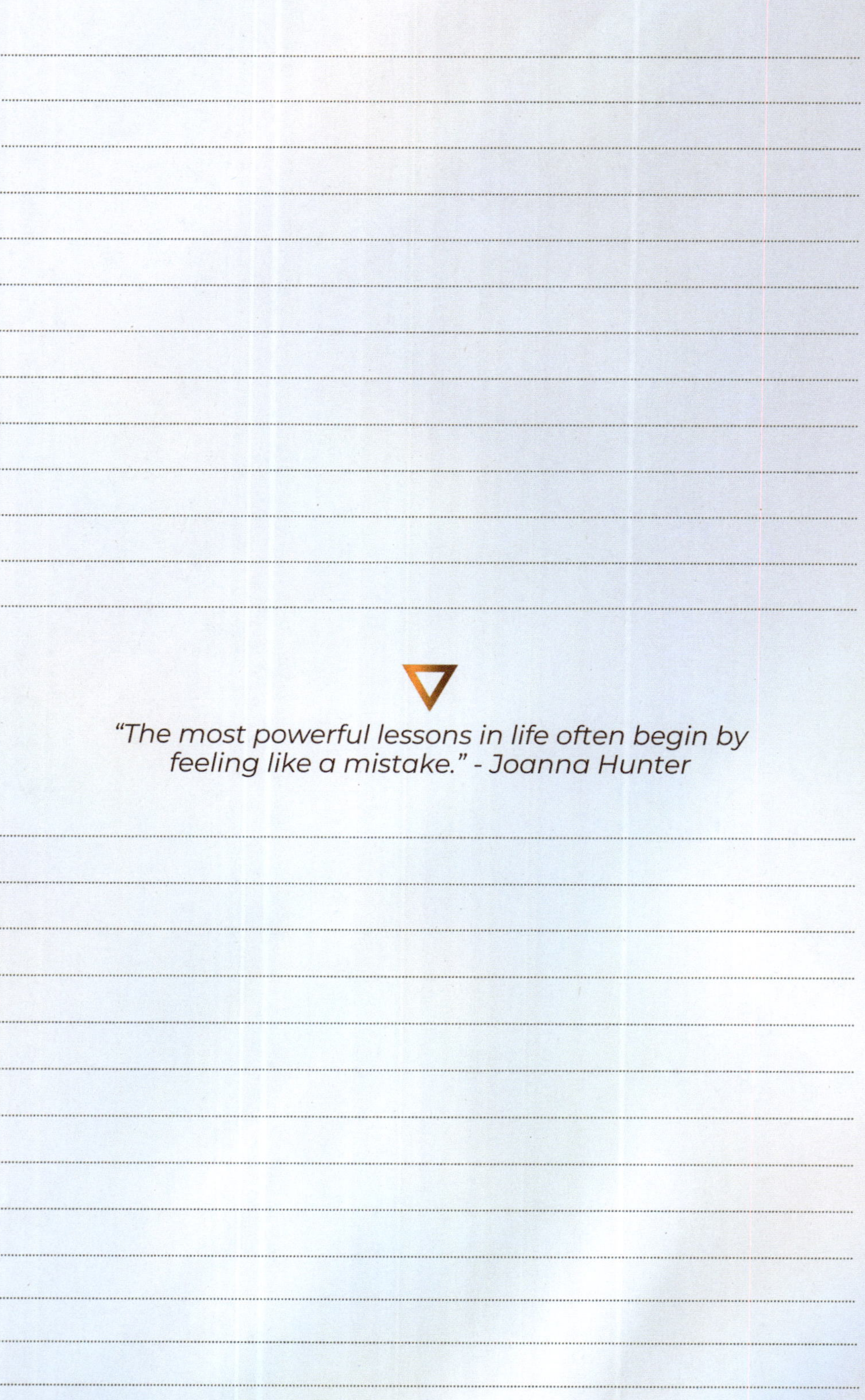
"The most powerful lessons in life often begin by feeling like a mistake." - Joanna Hunter

In gratitude, I acknowledge the serendipitous lessons that have given me these skills...

"Don't seek to erase errors of the past; learn from them instead."
- Anon

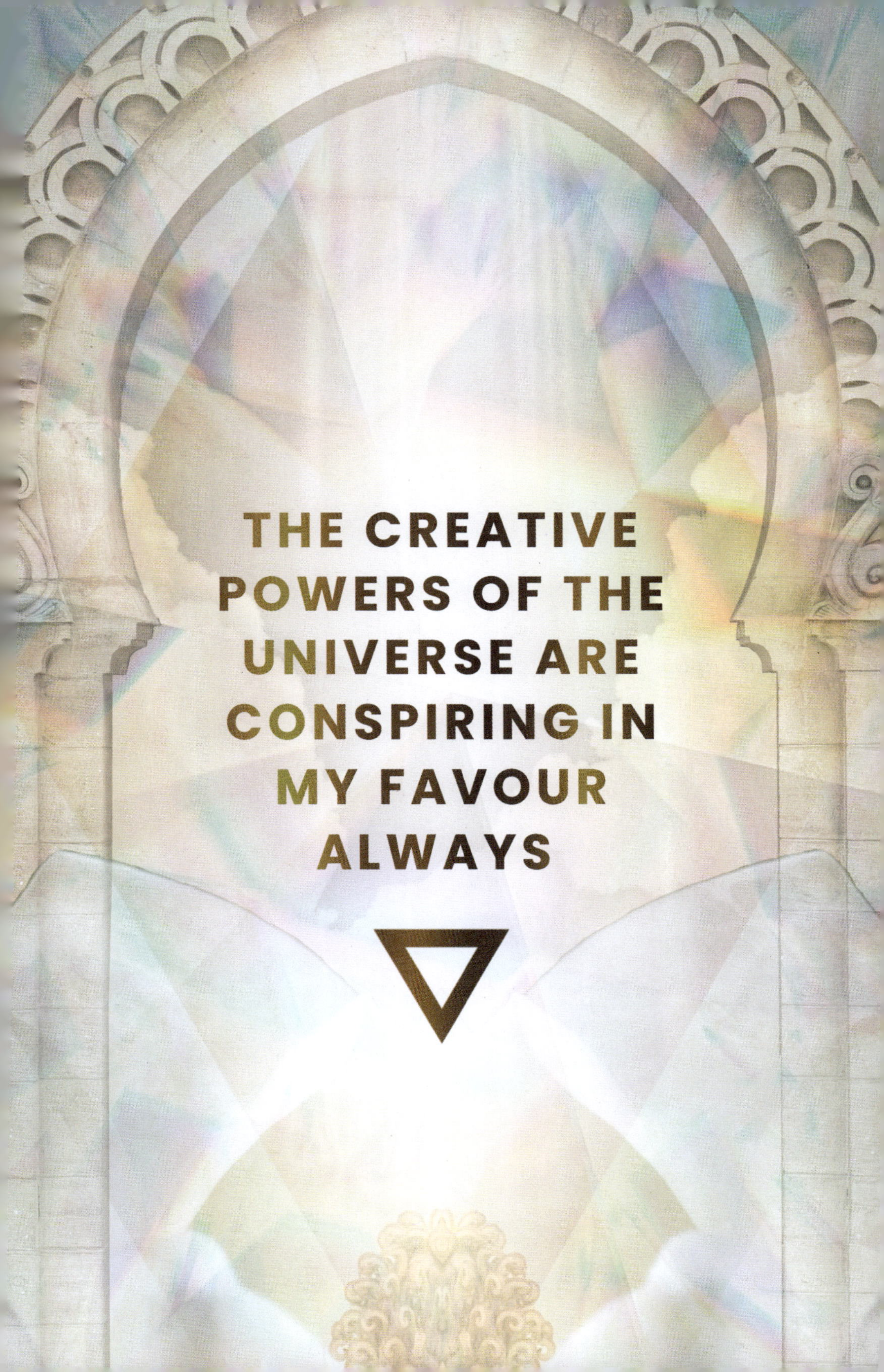
THE CREATIVE
POWERS OF THE
UNIVERSE ARE
CONSPIRING IN
MY FAVOUR
ALWAYS

My heart fills with gratitude and expands infinitely as I reflect with thankfulness on these lessons...

I open my heart and soul in the deepest gratitude to learning more life lessons that will give me...

"Life is 10% what happens to us and 90% how we react to it."
- Charles R. Swindoll

I choose this moment to fully appreciate the sacredness of these difficult life lessons...

"Education breeds confidence. Confidence breeds hope. Hope breeds peace." - Confucius

IT'S SAFE FOR
ME TO HAVE
EVERYTHING I
DESIRE

I am thankful for the intricate dance of life lessons, for in each step, I have found deeper meaning and a greater understanding of myself in these areas...

Gratitude fills my heart as I appreciate the life lessons and people that have been my guiding lights, illuminating the path of personal growth and self-discovery...

“Life is a succession of lessons which must be lived to be understood." - Helen Keller

Gratitude fills my soul as I reflect on the symphony of life lessons, each note contributing to the melody of my evolving self in this way...

“Every day is a school day on Earth, a new opportunity to learn.” - Skylar

ALL THAT I DESIRE IN
LIFE IS ALREADY
WITHIN ME AND
READY TO BE
EXPRESSED

Expressing deep thanks for the mosaic of learning that has led me to this...

Thankful for the kaleidoscope of my greatest life lesson...

"I am so grateful for every life lesson. Through them I got to know myself, and through knowing myself I got to appreciate the divine and see myself anew." - Joanna Hunter

As I pen down my thoughts in this divine now, I am grateful for the spiritual lessons unfolding, shaping my journey with purpose and grace...

“Sometimes you win, sometimes you learn." - John C. Maxwell

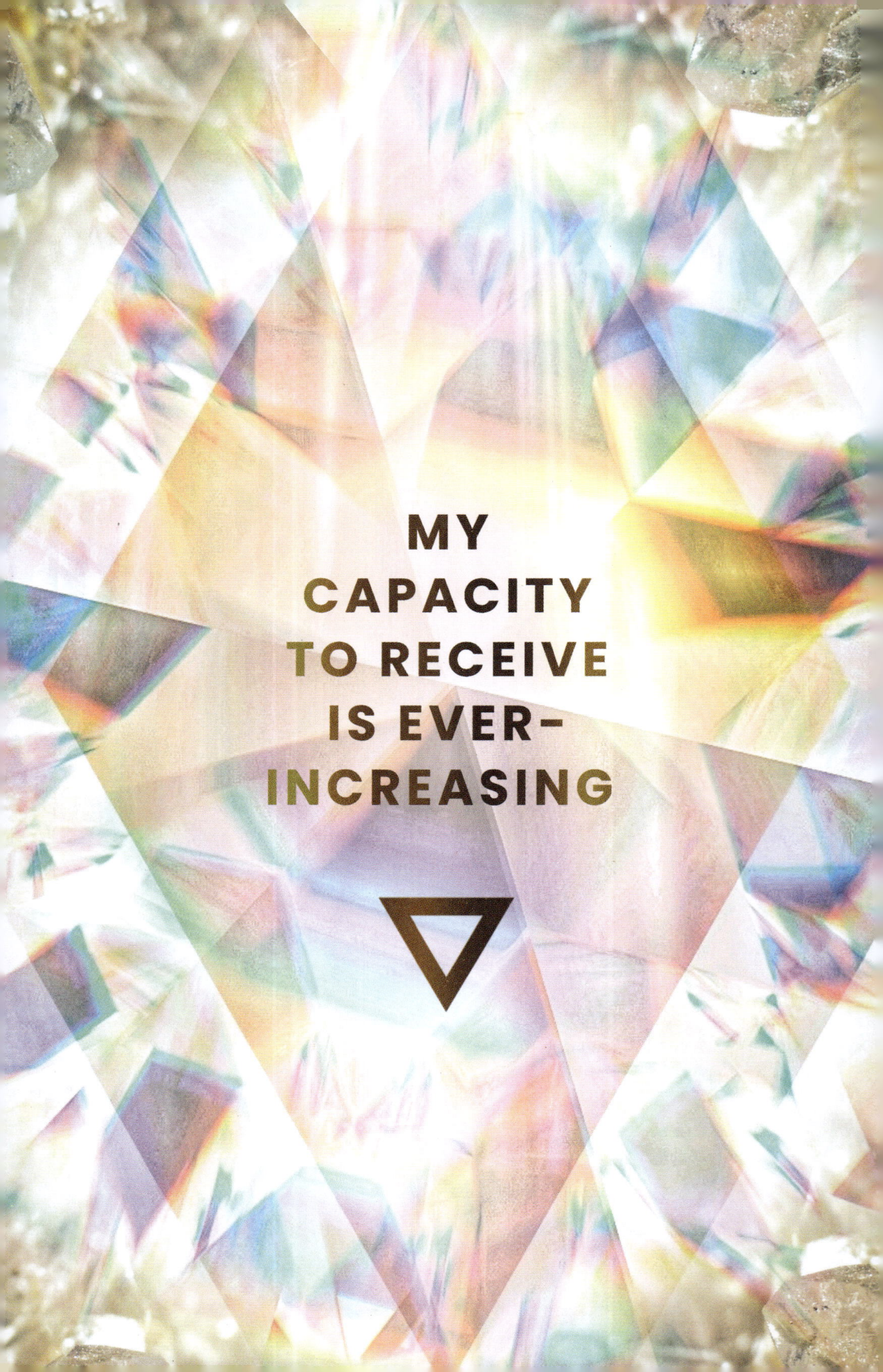
MY
CAPACITY
TO RECEIVE
IS EVER-
INCREASING

I am so awed by my grateful heart I got to learn this...

In the sacred dance of now, I extend my gratitude to the universe for the spiritual lessons woven into the fabric of this moment, elevating my consciousness...

"Learning is a treasure that will follow its owner everywhere."
- Chinese Proverb

With a heart brimming with gratitude, I celebrate the lessons engraved in the chapters of my past, shaping me into the resilient and compassionate soul I am today...

“I am always doing that which I cannot do, in order that I may learn how to do it." - Pablo Picasso

I AM SO LOVED.
MONEY LOVES
ME. LIFE LOVES
ME. SOURCE
LOVES ME

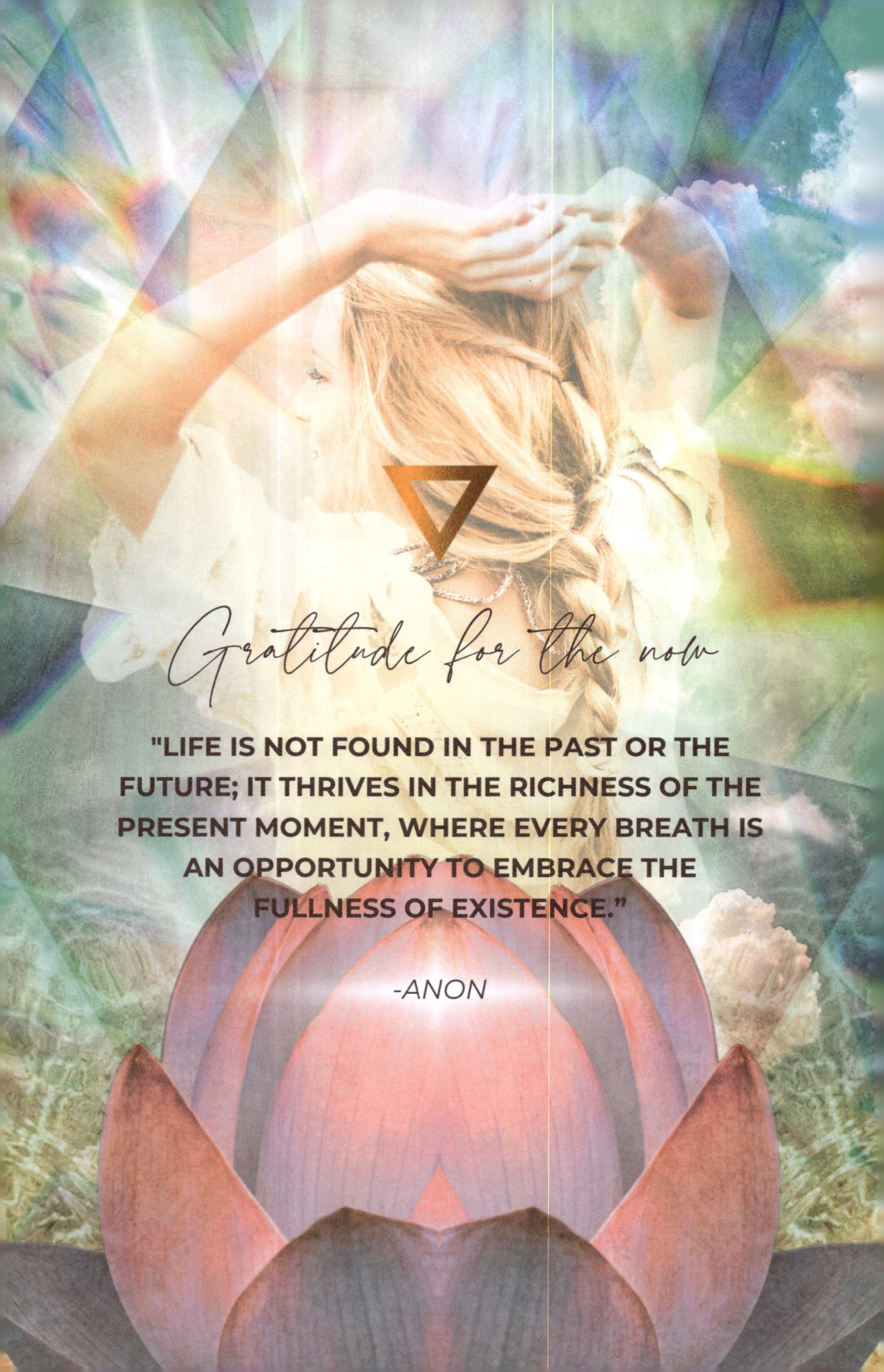

Gratitude for the now

"LIFE IS NOT FOUND IN THE PAST OR THE FUTURE; IT THRIVES IN THE RICHNESS OF THE PRESENT MOMENT, WHERE EVERY BREATH IS AN OPPORTUNITY TO EMBRACE THE FULLNESS OF EXISTENCE."

-ANON

Hey Daily Light Seeker,

Hold the phone because the NOW is our place of power! In this section, we are exploring the now through the lens of gratitude and presence.

In the rich tapestry of your existence, the present moment is a thread of divine power waiting to be woven into the fabric of your reality. Yet, in our busy lives it's easy to get entangled in the threads of past regrets or future worries, inadvertently overlooking the brilliance of the now. Imagine the untapped potential residing in each moment, a reservoir of energy waiting for you to dip into and shape the narrative of your life. Gratitude becomes the alchemy that transmutes the ordinary into the extraordinary, allowing you to harness the latent power of the now.

I have a little secret to share about the now moment, a life hack if you will. Most of the time fear does not inhabit the now moment, it's invited by virtue of filling your now with future worries which can cause fear-based anxiety or filling your now with thoughts of the past which can cause depressive thoughts... but if you still your mind and ask right here, right now, "Am I okay?" not 10 seconds from now but right this very second, "Am I okay?"- I promise the answer is almost always yes. There is pure power there as your now moment creates your next moment, but the time will always be now.

Joanna x X

▽

With an open heart, I embrace the gift of today with the most heartfelt gratitude...

Dear Universe, as I immerse myself in the now, I am profoundly grateful for the spiritual awakening that unfolds with each breath and heartbeat...

"The present moment holds infinite riches beyond your wildest dreams." - Earl Nightingale

Dear Divine, as I write in this journal I give thanks for...

"The present moment is a gift. Thank you for unwrapping it with gratitude." - Anon

TODAY,
WONDERFUL
THINGS WILL
UNFOLD FOR ME

In this sacred moment, I bow to the divine wisdom that guides me, expressing heartfelt gratitude for the richness of my now moment...

Divine Source, in the sanctuary of the present, I offer my gratitude for the lessons whispered in the winds of now, guiding me towards spiritual growth...

“The present moment is a powerful goddess."
- Johann Wolfgang von Goethe

I pause to appreciate the sacredness of now, acknowledging the divine lessons that shape my spiritual evolution...

“The present moment is the only moment available to us, and it is the door to all moments." - Thich Nhat Hanh

I AM SO LUCKY,
EVERYTHING IS
ALWAYS WORKING
OUT IN MY FAVOUR

Dear Universe, in the embrace of this present moment, I offer my deepest thanks for the divine presence that surrounds and fills me...

In the stillness of this NOW moment, I open my heart to the divine energy that flows through me, expressing gratitude for these spiritual insights which are now revealed to me...

"In this moment, I am grateful for the beauty that surrounds me and the blessings that fill my life." - Anon

Today, I surrender to the divine rhythm of life, expressing my deepest thanks for the spiritual gifts woven into the tapestry of this now moment...

"The NOW moment is where your power lives." - Skylar

I LOVE BEING
IN ALIGNMENT
TO THE BEST
VERSION OF ME

In this sacred space of journaling, I surrender to the divine flow of the present, thanking the universe for the spiritual blessings in my life...

In the silence of this moment, I connect with the divine essence within and express gratitude for all that I have in life...

"Gratitude can transform common days into thanksgivings, turn routine jobs into joy, and change ordinary opportunities into blessings." - William Arthur Ward

I express my gratitude for the insights that illuminate my path, unveiling the profound mysteries of my existence...

"Life gives you plenty of time to do whatever you want to do if you stay in the present moment." - Deepak Chopra

I AM ENOUGH

As I anchor my awareness in with gratitude into the sacred now, I am grateful for the divine whispers that guide me, shaping my spiritual journey with love and grace...

As I reflect on this moment, I am grateful for the divine synchronicities that guide me on my spiritual path, weaving its magic into my now moments...

"The art of life is to live in the present moment."
- Emmet Fox

In the gentle embrace of this moment, I surrender to the divine flow of existence, expressing deep gratitude for the spiritual lessons woven into the fabric of my present experience...

"Live so fully present in your now moment that it gives the universe
no alternative but to give you more incredible now moments.
Gratitude is the sacred key that unlocks this." - Joanna Hunter

MY GRATEFUL
HEART IS A MAGNET
FOR MIRACLES AND
OPENS ALL DOORS

Gratitude for what we are calling in
"BE THE CHANGE THAT YOU WISH TO SEE IN THE WORLD."
-MAHATMA GANDHI

Hey, Magic Maker, what are you calling in for your future?

Get excited because we are about to get down to some serious manifesting hi-jinks! Close your eyes and take a deep breath, imagine the catalogue of the universe is spread out before you, its pages are adorned with every imaginable thing possible, from mind-blowing experiences to states of energy like vitality to better-than-you-can-imagine creations for your life.... Best of all, you get to choose whatever you want from the catalogue of the universe!

Affirmations are a sacred and powerful way to reprogram your mind and place orders from the catalogue of the universe. When combined with gratitude they become a supercharged manifesting tool, one that I have effectively used to create my life design and order anything I desire from the catalogue of the universe.

In this journal you will find some of my favourite affirmations for creating amazing shifts in your life and calling in the most expansive realities for yourself. In the back of this journal I have ways to work with affirmations and how to create your own.

Joanna xX

In the sacred realm of future creation, I express gratitude for the divine abundance flowing into my life for these things...

Dear Source, in this moment of future manifestation, I express heartfelt gratitude for the abundance, joy, and spiritual alignment that are making their way into my life in these forms...

“Gratitude is a lens by which your life can heal in miraculous ways.” - Joanna Hunter

Dear Universe, as I set my intentions for the future, I am already grateful for...

" A grateful heart opens many doors within this cosmos."
- Skylar

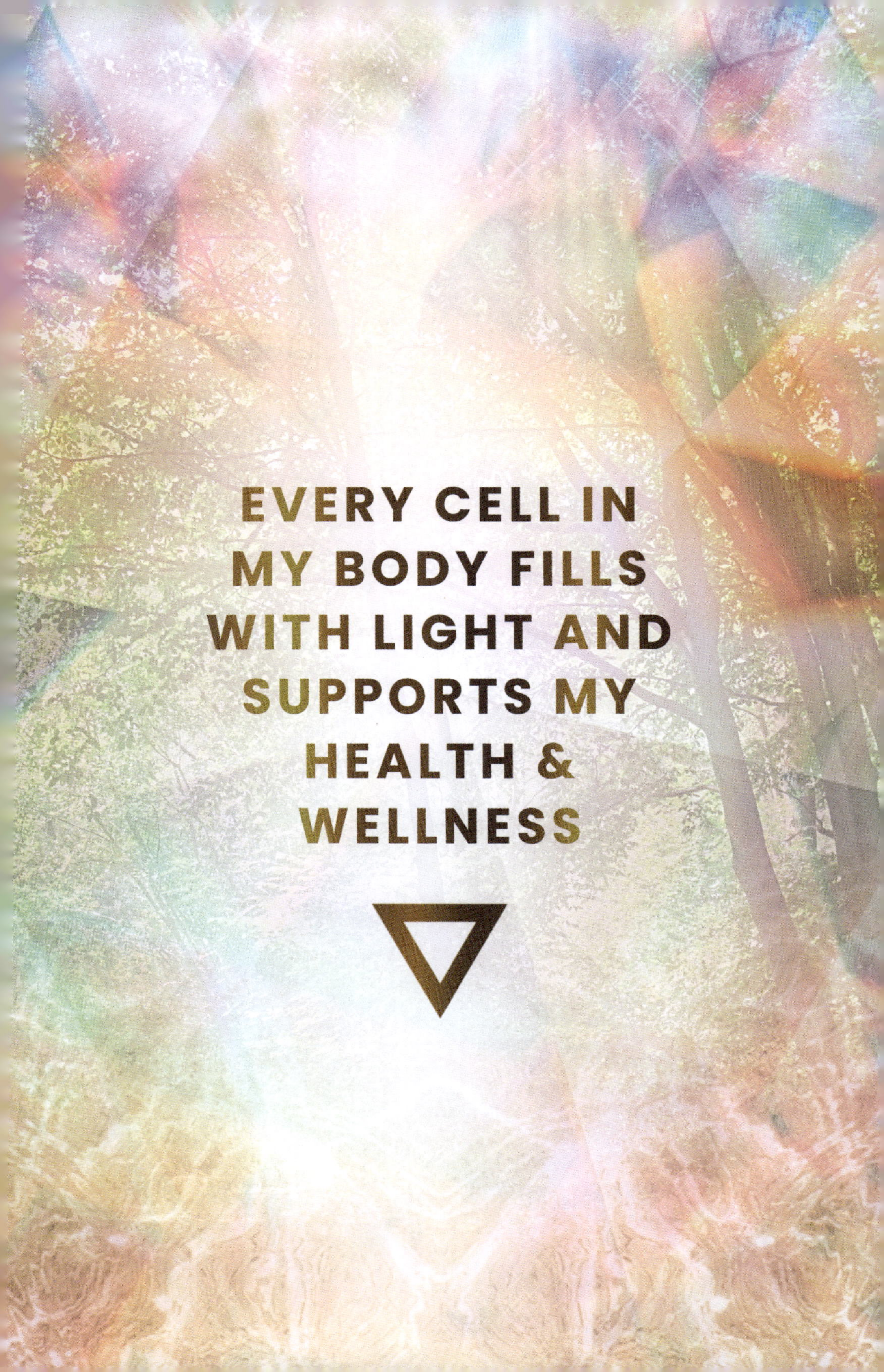
EVERY CELL IN
MY BODY FILLS
WITH LIGHT AND
SUPPORTS MY
HEALTH &
WELLNESS

In this sacred journal, I call forth the divine energies that will shape my future... give gratitude for these things...

In this sacred dialogue with the universe, I express gratitude for the divine plan that is intricately unfolding in these ways...

"Gratitude is the healthiest of all human emotions. The more you express gratitude for what you have, the more likely you will have even more to express gratitude for." - Zig Ziglar

In this sacred space of intention setting, I speak prophecy into my world and make manifest these things...

"The more grateful I am, the more beauty I see." - Mary Davis

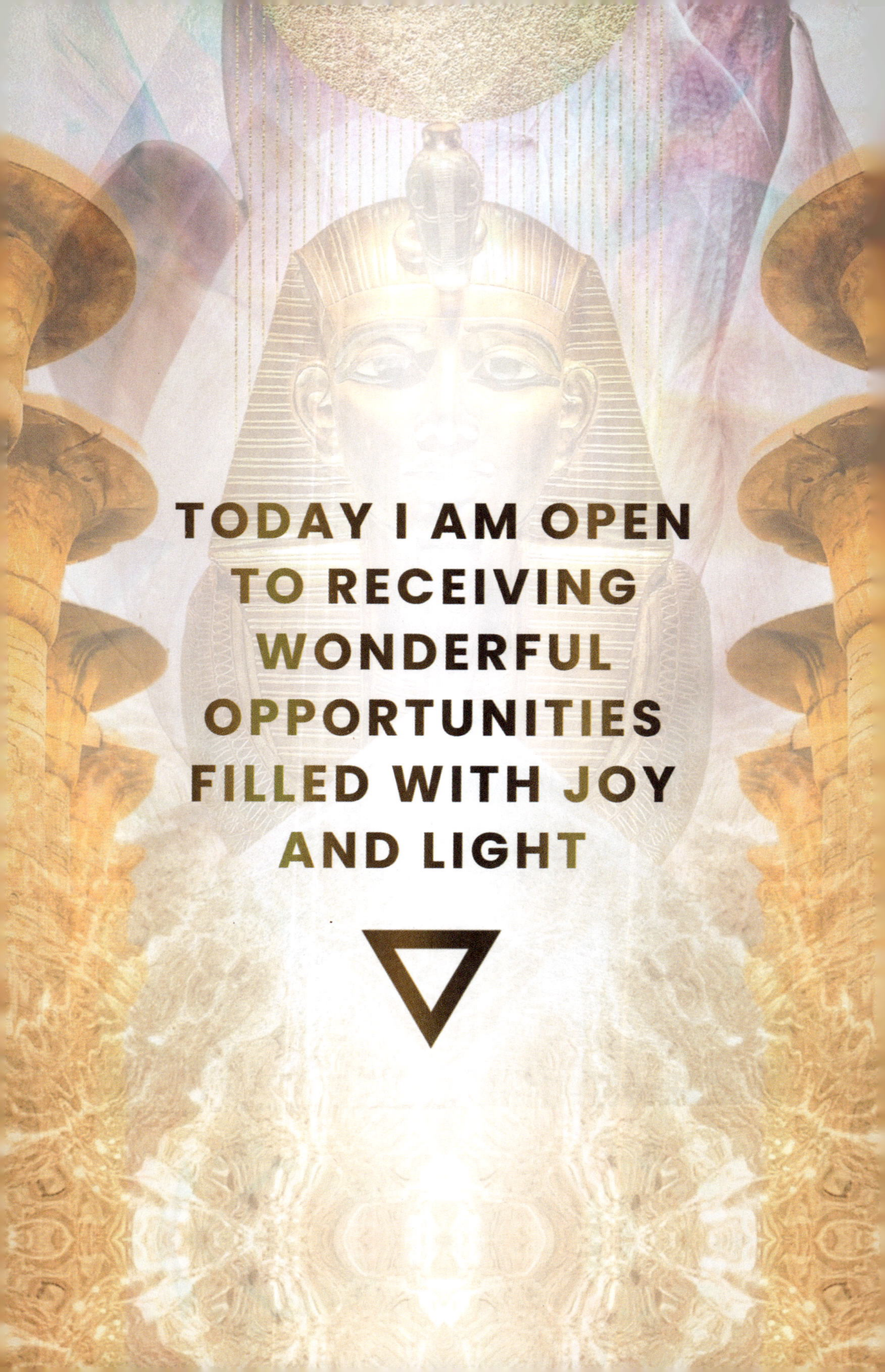
TODAY I AM OPEN
TO RECEIVING
WONDERFUL
OPPORTUNITIES
FILLED WITH JOY
AND LIGHT

Dear Spirit guides, as I cast my vision into the future, I am thankful for your unwavering support in...

As I write down my future desires, I am filled with gratitude for the spiritual energy that will guide my path and manifest my intentions into reality...

"What you think, you become. What you feel, you attract. What you imagine, you create." - Buddha

As I envision the future I wish to create, I am filled with gratitude for the divine guidance that will lead me, and the miracles that will manifest effortlessly...

"Gratitude is a powerful process for shifting your energy and bringing more of what you want into your life." - Rhonda Byrne

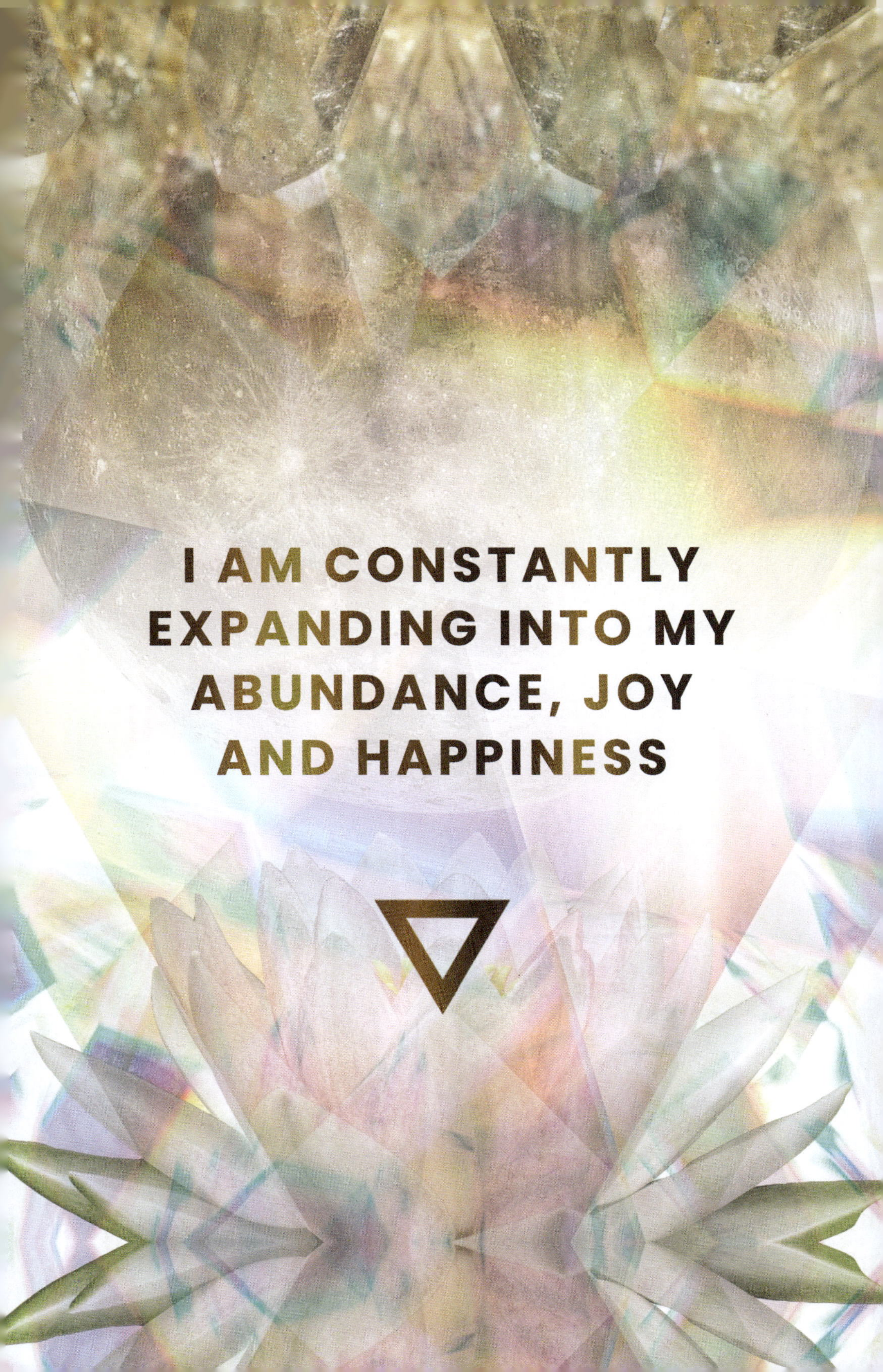
I AM CONSTANTLY
EXPANDING INTO MY
ABUNDANCE, JOY
AND HAPPINESS

Dear Universe, with a heart full of gratitude, I anticipate the divine manifestations that will grace my future, aligning with the abundance and joy I am calling forth...

As I journal my dreams for the future, I am grateful for the divine support that will pave the way and support me...

“Be thankful for what you have; you'll end up having more. If you concentrate on what you don't have, you will never, ever have enough." - Oprah Winfrey

In this sacred moment of co-creation, I express deep gratitude for the divine blessings already in motion to deliver...

EVERYTHING
IS POSSIBLE
FOR ME

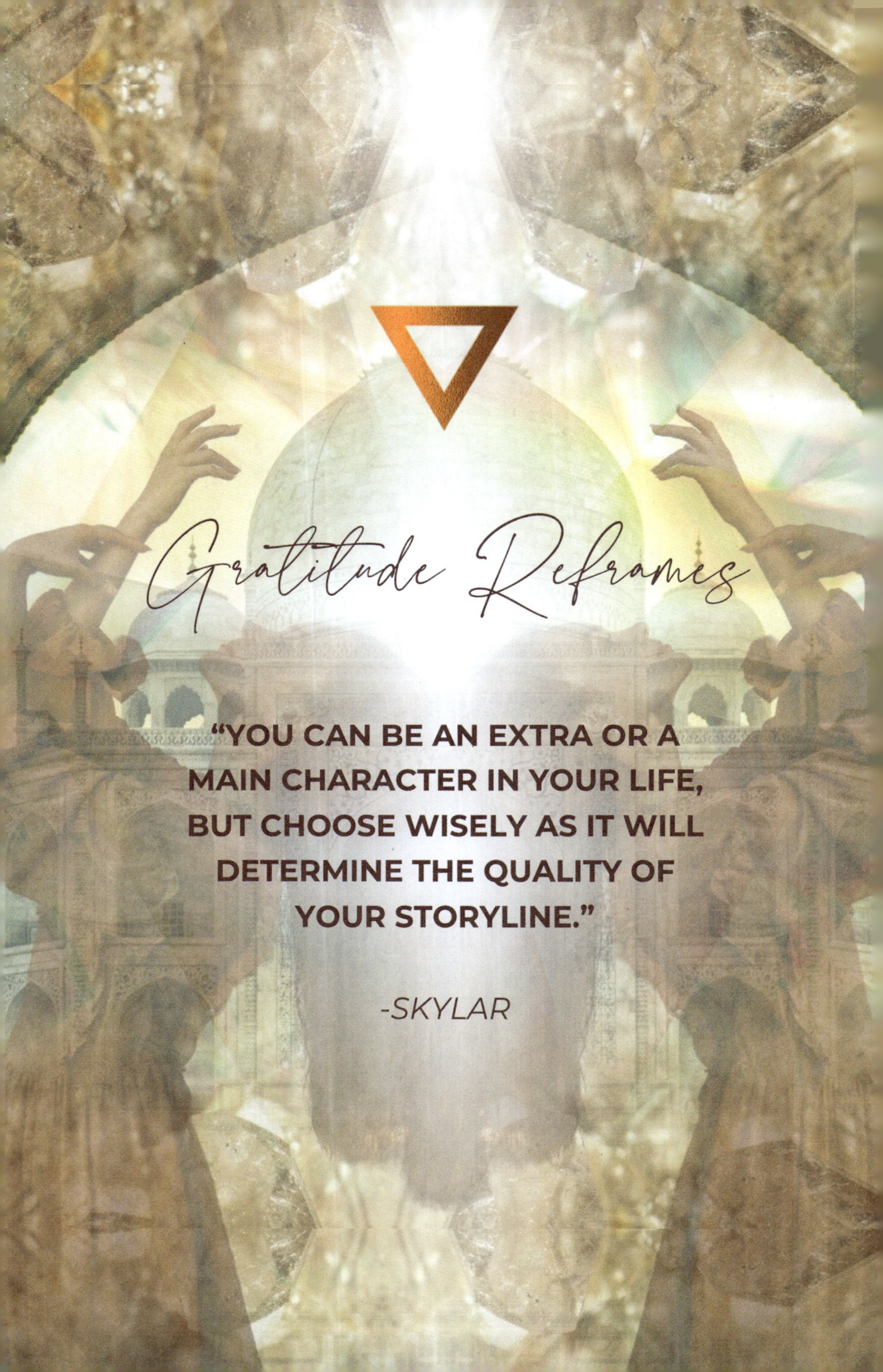
Gratitude Reframes
"YOU CAN BE AN EXTRA OR A MAIN CHARACTER IN YOUR LIFE, BUT CHOOSE WISELY AS IT WILL DETERMINE THE QUALITY OF YOUR STORYLINE."
-SKYLAR

Dear Sacred Soul,

I think you will love this one. I love using gratitude to reframe energy and amp up my personal power at the same time. The next time you feel like apologising, could you use gratitude instead? For example, switch "I am sorry I am late." to "Thank you for your patience." Or how about using gratitude to decline what you are not available for; "Thank you so much for thinking of me, however at this time I am at capacity for what I can do."

Reframes plus gratitude are a powerful combination that will help you shift your energy and align it with your deepest desires and of course more Daily Light. Could you reframe your way to better and brighter future timelines?

In the art of gratitude, I reframe any challenges as opportunities for growth, expressing thanks for the wisdom they have brought me...

In the canvas of my life, I reframe hardships as strokes of resilience, each one adding depth to the masterpiece of my journey...

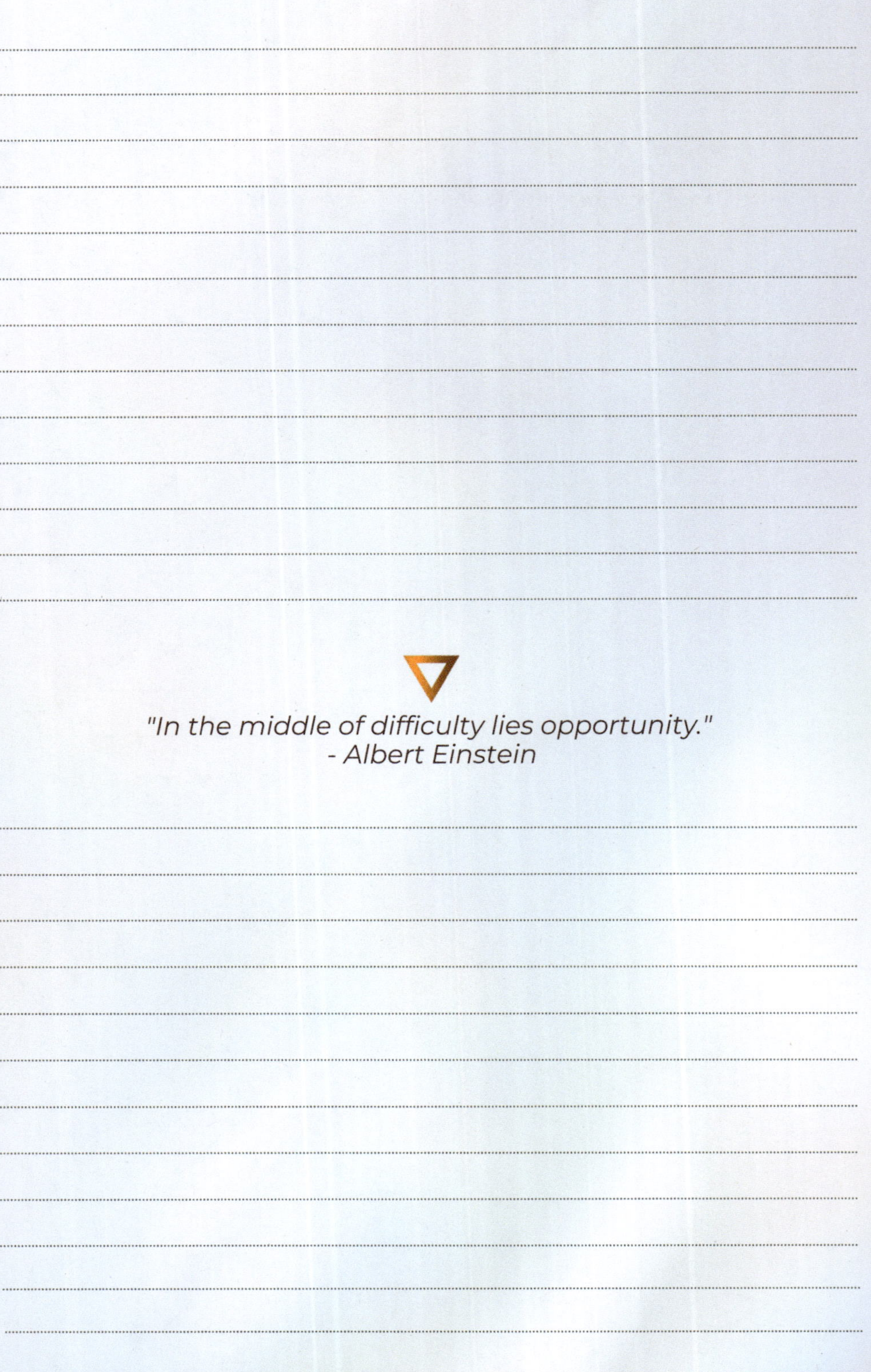
"In the middle of difficulty lies opportunity."
- Albert Einstein

Dearest heart with gratitude as my guide, I reframe uncertainties as opportunities for adventure...

"You are your best thing." - Toni Morrison

I AM A UNIQUE
EXPRESSION OF PURE
SOURCE ENERGY,
MAGNETIC TO MY
DESIRES AND INFINITE
IN MY LIGHT

With a heart full of gratitude, I reframe setbacks as stepping stones, acknowledging the valuable lessons they carry...

Expressing gratitude for the gift of perspective, I reframe difficulties as invitations to discover my strength and inner resources...

"Your beliefs become your thoughts, your thoughts become your words, your words become your actions, your actions become your habits, your habits become your values, and your values become your destiny." - Mahatma Gandhi

With a mindset of gratitude, I reframe obstacles as doorways and portals to transformation, recognizing the potential for positive change...

"Attitude is a little thing that makes a big difference." - Winston Churchill

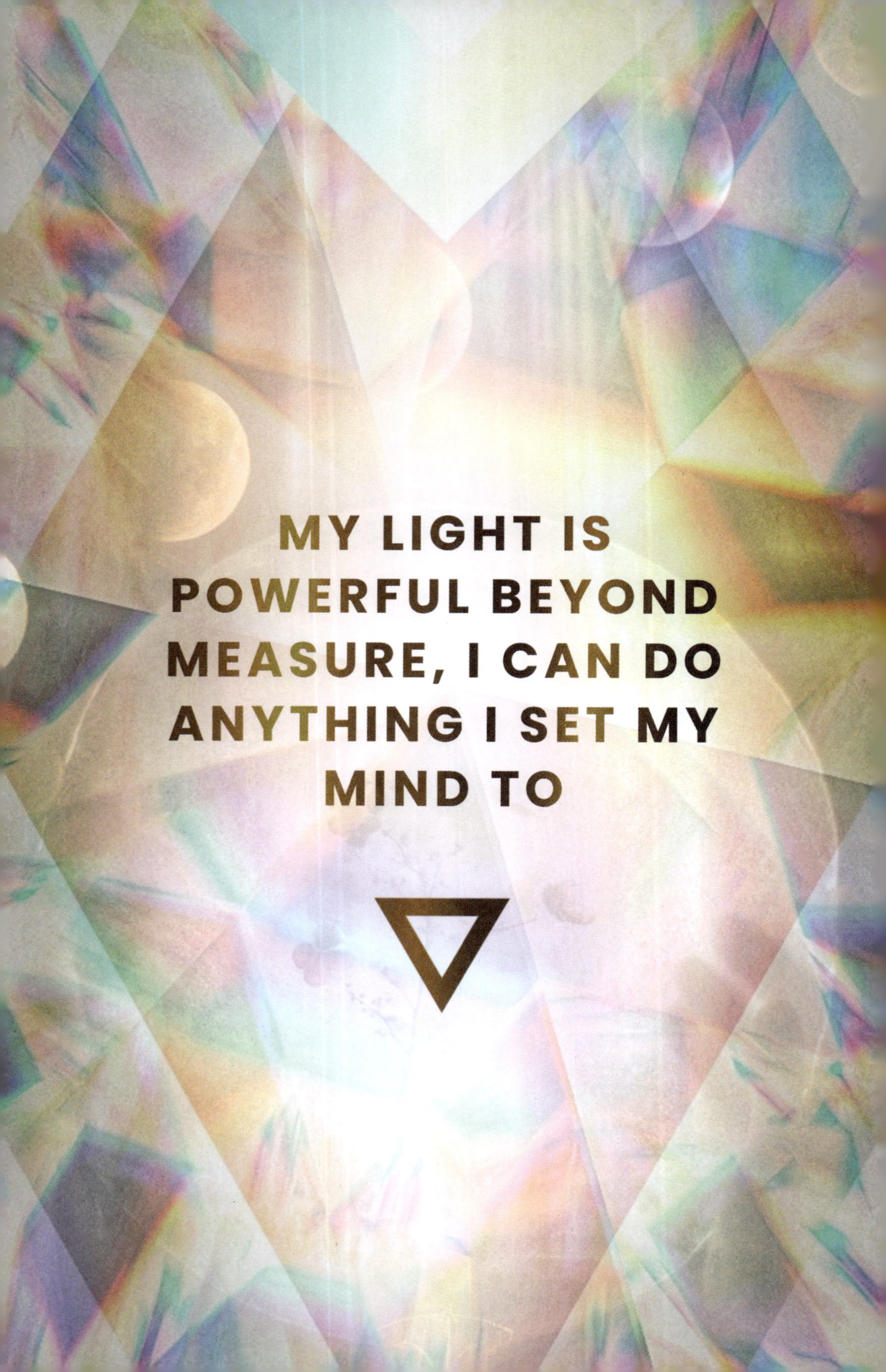
MY LIGHT IS
POWERFUL BEYOND
MEASURE, I CAN DO
ANYTHING I SET MY
MIND TO

In the dance of gratitude, I reframe difficulties as the rhythm that propels me forward, thankful for the beat that shapes my journey...

With gratitude as my guide, I reframe challenges as catalysts for transformation, embracing the blessings they have unfolded...

"Success is liking yourself, liking what you do, and liking how you do it." - Maya Angelou

Acknowledging my power of gratitude, I reframe endings as beginnings, grateful for the fresh new chapters they bring...

"Change the way you look at things, and the things you look at change."
- Wayne Dyer

I AM THE ANSWERED PRAYER OF MY PAST ME, AND THE VERSION OF ME MY FUTURE SELF IS PROUD OF, ALL IN THIS NOW MOMENT

In the language of thankfulness, I reframe mistakes as lessons, appreciating the growth that comes from embracing my perfect imperfections...

Expressing thanks for the grace of gratitude, I reframe setbacks as setups for comebacks...

"You are both the receiver and perceiver of your life experience - how you tell the story of your life matters." - Skylar

Dearest Universe, in the spirit of appreciation, I reframe losses as gains in experience...

"Man is not disturbed by events, but by the view he takes of them."
-Epictetus

ABUNDANCE FLOWS
TO ME IN EVER-
INCREASING
AMOUNTS

"Choose success, choose it so hard that the universe has no other option but to deliver it." - Joanna Hunter

How to use affirmations

If you are not really sure how to use affirmations, start by repeating them as many times as you can. A great tip is to do this when you are doing repetitive tasks or tasks where you don't have to think too much, like cleaning or when at the gym. Our brains are often very receptive when we do the mundane so adding an affirmation during these tasks will take advantage of this receptive state and add some daily light in otherwise dull tasks.

The game of *Liar Ping Pong.*

Now you might become aware of a game of Liar Ping Pong starting to play out in your head. It goes like this: "I am so healthy." you say, and your mind pipes up "Liar! You just ate cheese-loaded nachos." However the affirmation **"I am so healthy." is actually the reality you want.**

As I see it, you have three options:

Option one - Cry into your nachos and order the thick shake because you are doomed to become a health failure!

Option two - You realise you are the creator of your reality and you will be having that healthy reality thank you very much, despite the nachos you just ate. So you keep going with, "I am so healthy.", knowing that the negative voice is also the weaker voice inside you and you will eventually silence it as it is inherently lazy and will give up; that is its nature.

Option three - Outsmart the negative voice by only saying statements that are true. Instead of "I am so healthy." where you might encounter resistance, use "I love feeling healthy." Just try it. Can you feel the difference in energy? No resistance, right? Because what you said was true.

Don't be afraid to modify the affirmations to suit you better as the universe gives us more of what we give attention to. Focusing on 'healthy', especially with the feeling and energy of love, will increase it in your life. "I love..." - followed by the statement you want to be true is a great hack for affirmations because you are less likely to encounter your own resistance. Less resistance = faster results.

Two ways I love to use affirmations:

Heart centred way: I say the affirmation then imagine it in my heart radiating out. I place my hands over my heart and breathe in the affirmation; I really imagine the statement is true. This creates a powerful shift within me that I wrap my energy in.

The affirmation shower: I say the affirmation, repeating it again and again as I imagine the words like a shower of source energy; bright golden-white light coming through my head/crown chakra permeating every cell of my body, adjusting, correcting and loving the cells into the frequency of my affirmation, powerfully shifting my frequency to emit this new frequency. The shower is cleansing away the old energy, and filling my cells with the new affirmation. As I do this I imagine the affirmation to be soooooo true and what my life would be like in this new reality.

After doing this I always feel different and more aligned to the affirmation.

Feel free to make your own affirmations, but be mindful of only giving attention to that which you want more of. In the spirit of understanding, "I want to be debt free." does not make a good affirmation. The intention of the affirmation is good, however, the wording will leave you in debt. As debt is a non-negotiable word it has one meaning and one meaning only; it means you owe something. If you focus on it, you will bring more of it to you.

A better affirmation would be "I love having financial freedom." This statement will bring you the energy of financial freedom, which is ultimately what is desired in this scenario.

Here are a few other examples of better ways to word your affirmations for greater success.

I am pain free → I love how my body moves with ease & joy

I am losing weight → I am my perfect size & shape

I am never late → I am always on time

The key to affirmations working is to use them regularly and to be consistent. I have had many people tell me affirmations don't work, but upon further investigation I discover that, if they don't become skinny or wealthy in thirty six or so hours, they stop using them!

So I will leave you with the immortal words of Zig Ziglar as this quote works for affirmations too!

"Positive thinking is like bathing; for it to be most effective, we recommend you do it daily." -Zig Ziglar

About Joanna & Skylar

Step into the enchanting world of Joanna Hunter and the collective consciousness Skylar, where metaphysical science meets everyday magic for real world application.

Joanna Hunter, is Metaphysical Teacher, Author, International Speaker, and the High Priestess of the transformative LightWeb® teachings. In her spiritual journey, Joanna created the world's largest metaphysical experiment, My Million Dollar Experiment, challenging the status quo and inviting light seekers to join her movement of conscious millionaires and change makers.

Joanna shares her life's stories intertwined with deep metaphysical truths to catalyse the awakening of the best versions of her audience. Skylar, the millions-strong collective consciousness she channels, are the unincarnated members of Joanna's soul tribe, who channel the Codex of Light™ a spiritual guide for human ascension teachings directly to her. Their mission is to assist in the ascension of humanity, bringing back YOUnity to Earth and dispelling suffering by rekindling the magic of our own soul's truth.

Gratitude is Joannas all time favourite spiritual practice for deep transformational change, alongside powerful affirmations it's a winning combination to create more Daily Light for you.

The profound wisdom imparted by Joanna and Skylar has guided thousands to align with their true selves, resulting in increased joy, fulfilment, and spiritual and material wealth.

If you would like further help using gratitude, affirmations or to learn about other LightTools™ Joanna has to change your life visit www.joannahunter.com

MUSE
ORACLE
PRESS
SCAN HERE
TO SEE MORE TITLES FROM
JOANNA HUNTER
MUSE
ORACLE
PRESS